D0688915

AMAZING BODY SYSTEMS
NERVOUS SYSTEM

by Karen Latchana Kenney

Ideas for Parents and Teachers

Pogo Books let children practice reading informational text while introducing them to nonfiction features such as headings, labels, sidebars, maps, and diagrams, as well as a table of contents, glossary, and index.

Carefully leveled text with a strong photo match offers early fluent readers the support they need to succeed.

Before Reading

- "Walk" through the book and point out the various nonfiction features. Ask the student what purpose each feature serves.
- Look at the glossary together. Read and discuss the words.

Read the Book

- Have the child read the book independently.
- Invite him or her to list questions that arise from reading.

After Reading

- Discuss the child's questions. Talk about how he or she might find answers to those questions.
- Prompt the child to think more. Ask: What other body systems do you know about? What do they do? How might they interact with the nervous system?

Pogo Books are published by Jump!
5357 Penn Avenue South
Minneapolis, MN 55419
www.jumplibrary.com

Copyright © 2017 Jump!
International copyright reserved in all countries. No part of this book may be reproduced in any form without written permission from the publisher.

Library of Congress Cataloging-in-Publication Data

Names: Kenney, Karen Latchana, author.
Title: Nervous system / by Karen Latchana Kenney.
Description: Minneapolis, MN: Jump!, Inc., [2017]
Series: Amazing body systems | Audience: Ages 7–10.
Includes bibliographical references and index.
Identifiers: LCCN 2016033550 (print)
LCCN 2016036327 (ebook)
ISBN 9781620315606 (hardcover: alk. paper)
ISBN 9781620316009 (pbk.)
ISBN 9781624965081 (ebook)
Subjects: LCSH: Nervous system—Juvenile literature.
Classification: LCC QP361.5 .K46 2017 (print)
LCC QP361.5 (ebook) | DDC 612.8—dc23
LC record available at https://lccn.loc.gov/2016033550

Series Editor: Jenny Fretland VanVoorst
Series Designer: Anna Peterson
Photo Researcher: Anna Peterson

Photo Credits: All photos by Shutterstock except: Alamy, 9; Dreamstime, 12-13; Getty, 6-7, 10-11, 14, 20-21, 23; iStock, 1.

Printed in the United States of America at Corporate Graphics in North Mankato, Minnesota.

33614080422271

TABLE OF CONTENTS

CHAPTER 1
IN CONTROL

Your body does a lot in a day.
You wake up. You breathe.
You eat, skip, and run.

You also know to stay away from things that hurt you. How does your body know what to do? The **nervous system** is in control. This system is in charge of sending messages through the body.

You move your legs, arms, fingers, and toes by choice. But this system also sends messages you don't know you're sending.

You breathe, blink, and move food through your body. You shiver when you're cold. You sweat when you're hot. The nervous system controls everything your body does.

TAKE A LOOK!

Your nervous system runs throughout your entire body.

brain

spinal cord

nerves

CHAPTER 2

. . . .

NERVE HIGHWAY

Your nervous system is made up of a highway of **nerves** that transmit messages through your body.

The **brain** and **spinal cord** are also parts of this system.

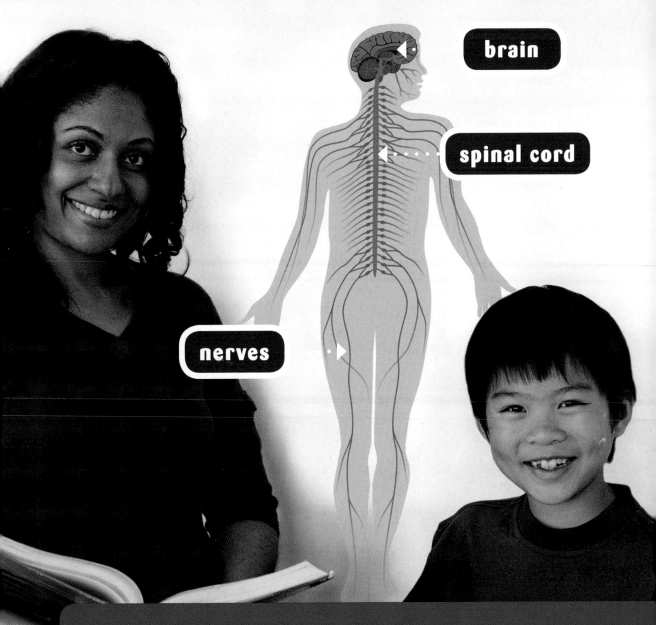

brain

spinal cord

nerves

The brain directs traffic. This **organ** is your thinking machine. Millions of **nerve cells** surround it. The hard bone of the skull protects the brain.

Nerves are long, connected threads of nerve cells. Some nerves branch off from the brain. They connect to parts of the head.

Most nerves travel down the spinal cord. It runs down your back. Hard **vertebrae** protect the nerves inside. These bones make up your spine.

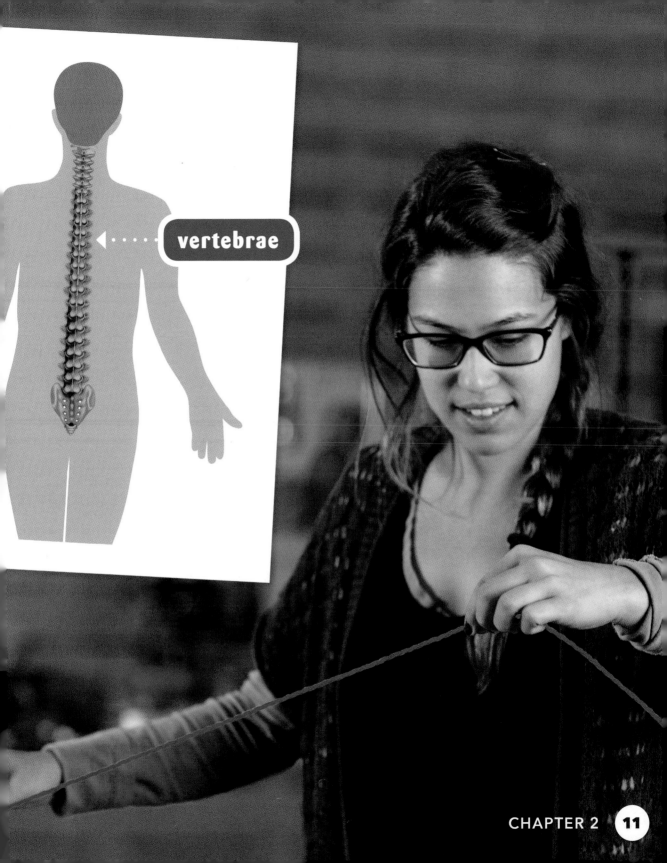

vertebrae

The nerves branch off in pairs from the cord. They become smaller and smaller. Some go to your arms, hands, legs, and feet. Other nerves connect with your lungs, heart, and other organs.

DID YOU KNOW?

You hear, see, taste, smell, and touch because of your nervous system. These are your senses. Messages move from your ears, eyes, mouth, nose, and skin to your brain. It's how you know about the world around you.

nerves

heart

CHAPTER 3

GET THE MESSAGE

Let's look at the nervous system in action.

Imagine you grab something hot.

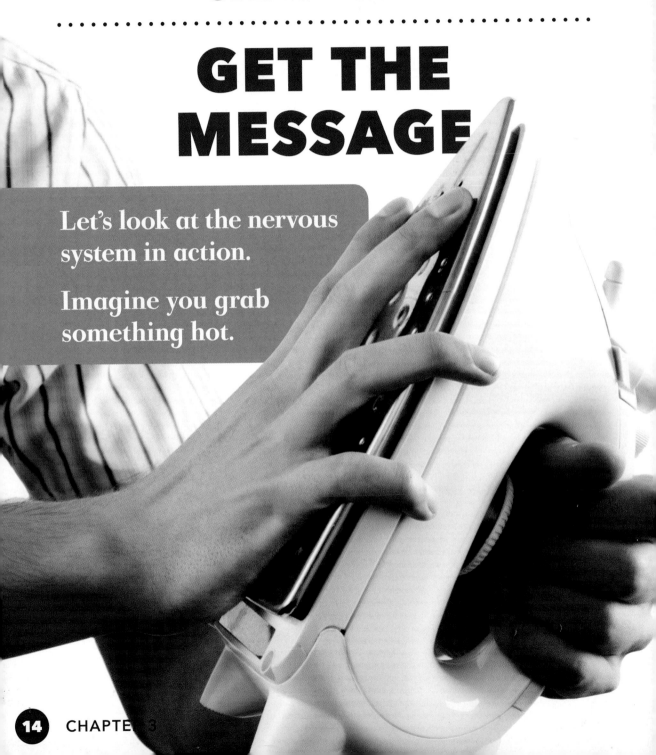

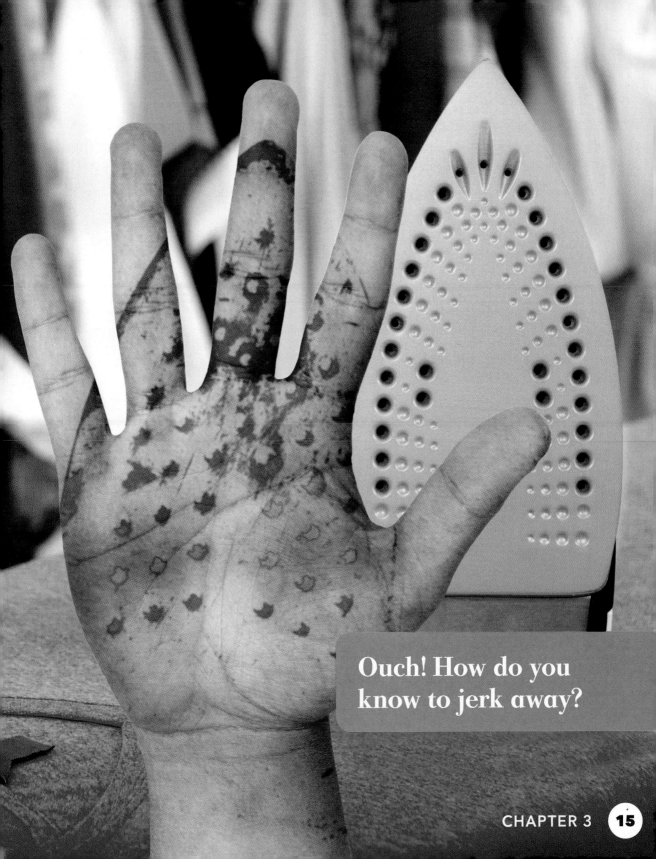

Ouch! How do you know to jerk away?

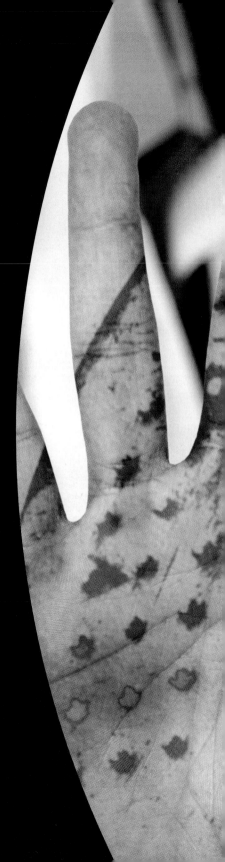

Your fingers are rich in nerve cells. First one of these cells makes an electric signal. It goes from end to end in the cell. Then the cell lets off a **chemical** signal. Now the message can jump to the next cell. These messages move fast, too! The fastest ones are faster than most racecars.

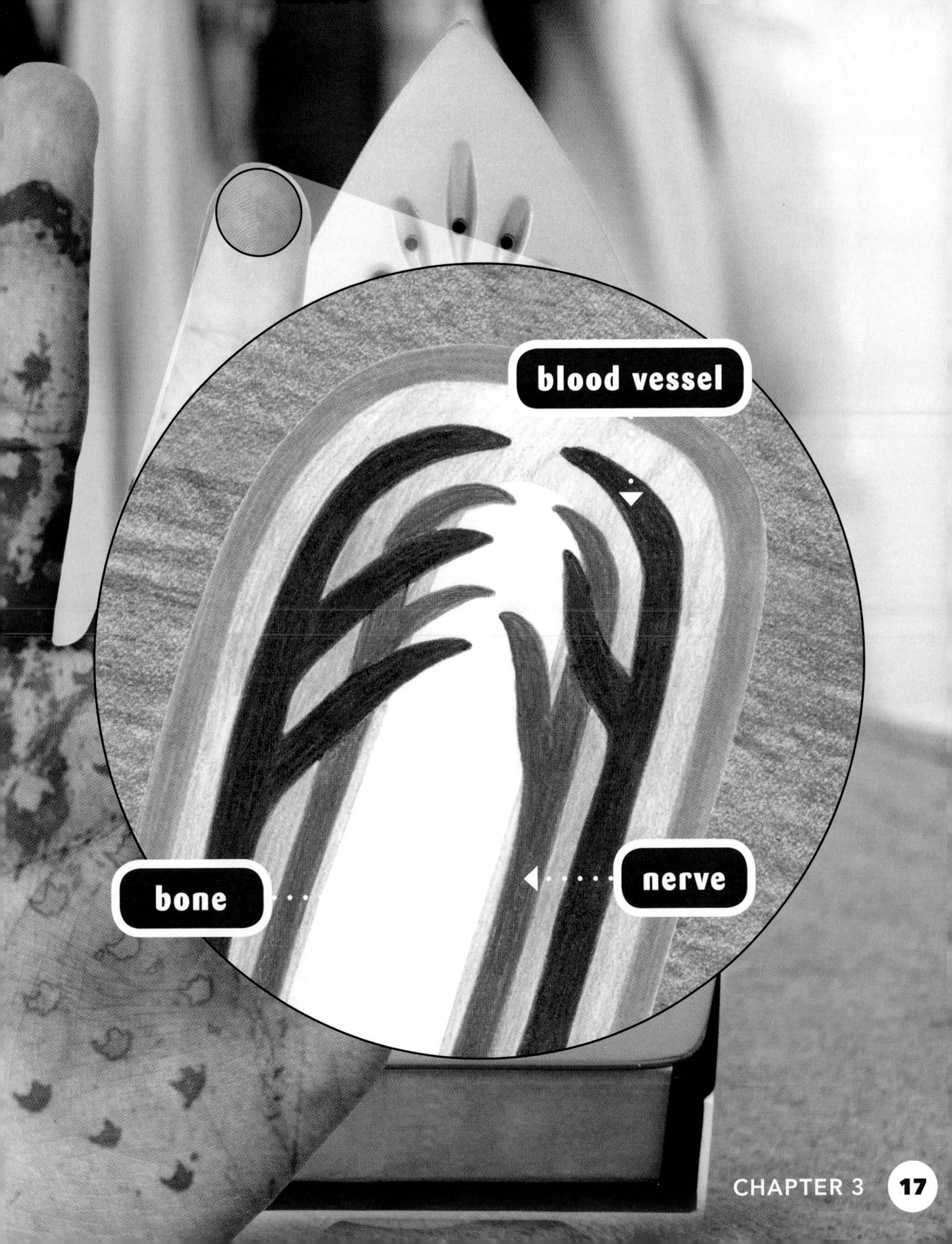
blood vessel
nerve
bone

The brain gets the message. In an instant it tells your body what to do. Hot! Let go!

You let go. You run your hands under cool water. Your nerves sense that, too.

Whew! Much better.

DID YOU KNOW?

In trouble? Your nervous system comes to the rescue! If you are afraid or in pain, a message goes to a **gland**. It releases a chemical. Your body gets a burst of energy. Now you can react to stay safe.

Your nervous system works with many other body systems. It controls your breath. It makes you move. It lets you see, hear, and taste, too. When it comes to your body, who's the boss? Your nervous system is.

ACTIVITIES & TOOLS

KNEE REFLEX

Send a message to your brain and watch your body react with a reflex.

You will need:

- your hand
- your leg
- a chair

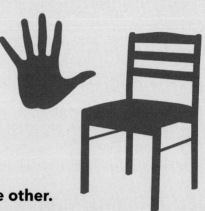

❶ Sit on a chair. Cross one leg over the other.

❷ Find the spot right below your kneecap. Hit it quickly with the side of your hand. Don't hit too hard! This sends a message to your brain.

❸ Watch your leg. What happens? Your brain's message causes your leg to kick out. This is a reflex.

GLOSSARY

brain: The organ inside your head that you use to think and feel.

chemical: Something made in the body that sends a signal.

gland: An organ that makes chemicals in the body.

nerve cells: Cells in the nervous system.

nerves: Threads of nerve cells.

nervous system: A body system that sends messages and controls action, organs, and senses.

organ: A part of the body that does a certain job.

spinal cord: A cord of nerves that runs down the spine and connects the brain to the body.

vertebrae: The small bones that make up the spine.

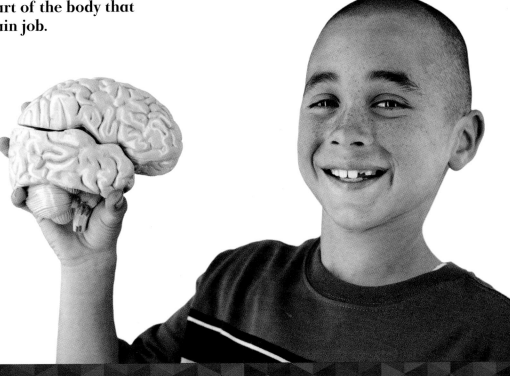

INDEX

TO LEARN MORE

Learning more is as easy as 1, 2, 3.

1) Go to www.factsurfer.com

2) Enter "nervoussystem" into the search box.

3) Click the "Surf" button to see a list of websites.

With factsurfer, finding more information is just a click away.